Mississippi Morning

Written by Ruth Vander Zee
Illustrated by Floyd Cooper

Eerdmans Books for Young Readers

Grand Rapids, Michigan • Cambridge, U.K.

Text ©2004 Ruth Vander Zee
Illustrations © 2004 Floyd Cooper

Published 2004 by Eerdmans Books for Young Readers
An imprint of Wm. B. Eerdmans Publishing Company
255 Jefferson S.E., Grand Rapids, Michigan 49503
P.O. Box 163, Cambridge CB3 9PU U.K.

04 05 06 07 08 09 10   7   6   5   4   3   2   1

ISBN 0-8028-5211-4

A catalog record of this book is available from the Library of Congress.

The illustrations were rendered in oil on board.
The display type was set in Windsor and University.
The text type was set in Old Style 7.
Art Director Gayle Brown
Graphic Design Matthew Van Zomeren

To my husband, Vern — a man of honor
—*R. V. Z.*

For Ruth
—*F. C.*

"James William, I don't know how we could keep this place going without your help. You can go now, but you be sure you don't get into any trouble."

I wiped the sweat from my sunburned face and looked at Ma. She seemed to worry about trouble. I had no idea why. It was 1933 and life was good for me. Ma kept busy caring for my two younger sisters, her garden, and the few animals we still had. I did a lot of the chores early in the morning and then was free to roam in the woods near our place. The last thing I would ever want to do is put my ma's mind to worrying about anything.

Pa had rented out our land long ago and was busy in the hardware store he owned in town. Some afternoons I'd walk into town and help him. "Yep, this is my son," he'd brag to anyone within earshot. "He does all the chores at home so I can run this store."

I'd sweep the wooden floor and listen to my pa. It seemed that somebody was always stopping in at one time or other to talk to him. In fact, one afternoon one of those men walked over to where I was working and said, "You know, James William, most of the important decisions in our part of Mississippi are made right here on the porch of your papa's store."

I was proud when he said that. It seemed all the men in town respected my pa. They'd huddle together. They wondered about the weather. They worried how cotton prices were dropping. They remembered how good things used to be. Every now and then, they'd talk so low I couldn't hear what they were saying. They'd talk in troubled tones and wave their fingers at each other.

One day I asked my pa, "Why do they get so riled when they talk with each other?"

"Son, there are some things you just don't understand," Pa said sternly. "Times are hard right now. These are good men. They're trying their hardest to put food on the table for their families. But no matter how hard they work, they still don't have two nickels to rub together." He looked me straight in the eye. "James William, these men are trying to protect what little they have. A man's gotta do what he thinks is best for his family."

Thick woods surrounded our property. I roamed these
woods with Red who lived close by. Red's real name was
Charles but he'd been called Red ever since his hair came
in a fiery orange. I had been lucky enough to get a rifle for
my twelfth birthday, so we'd hunt raccoons and rabbits.
As we hunted, we'd swap stories. Sometimes we'd get to
exaggerating so much the truth of our stories was hard to
find. But Red got my attention real fast when he started
talking about what he heard his pa talking to my pa about
down at the store.

"Yep," he drawled. "I heard your pa telling my pa that colored preacher who lives on the way out of town got what was coming to him."

"What do you mean 'got what was coming to him'?" I asked. "His house burned by accident. It wasn't nobody's fault."

"Not according to what I heard," Red replied. "Your pa said that man had to be stopped from stirring up colored folk. Said he was tellin' them to register to vote. Then my pa said men like him were nothing but trouble and it was high time they learned their lesson."

"Are you telling me that somebody went and burned that house?" I asked. "Nobody would do that."

"Well, go ask your pa. I couldn't hear everything 'cause they were talking real quiet. But I'm sure I heard it right."

"I'm sure you heard it wrong," I answered.

Besides spending many long hours with Red that summer, I also spent time with LeRoy, whose family sharecropped on the land next to ours. LeRoy was the best fisherman around. On afternoons when I wanted to fish, I'd find LeRoy. He knew more about hooks, bait, and good fishing spots than anybody I knew. We always fished in secluded places where no one would notice us. My pa always spoke disparagingly about white folk spending time with colored folk. He said it wasn't natural.

One afternoon when the fish weren't biting, I said, "Hey, LeRoy, let's go fish under that tree over there. That looks like a good spot."

LeRoy didn't look at me. He didn't say anything for a long time. I thought maybe he hadn't heard me. Finally he spoke so as I almost missed it. "I don't want to fish there."

"Why?"

"'Cause that's the hanging tree."

"What in the world are you talking about?" I asked.

"That's where the Klan left a black man hangin' for a whole day because he did something they didn't like."

"The Klan?"

"Yeah. Those people who ride at night wearing their white robes and ugly pointed hoods. They're scary."

"I never heard of no Klan," I said.

"You may not have heard of the Klan, but my mama told me just the other night that they poured hot tar over a black man who talked to a white lady. They don't mess around. They took bullwhips to my friend's daddy."

"Are you sure?" I asked.

"Yeah, I'm sure. My daddy says that we black folks just have to be careful and mind our own business. That's why I don't tell him that I come fishin' with you. He wouldn't like it."

I thought about what LeRoy said for a long time. Somehow it didn't make sense to me. Whenever I went into town I saw colored men trading at my pa's store. They were very polite and called my pa "Sir." My pa was always friendly and said, "Now, Boy, you come back when you need something else."

Colored men and women traded in the five and dime all the time. They kept money in the bank and on some Saturdays were allowed to sit in the balcony of the theater to watch a movie. This all seemed normal to me. It's true that they couldn't drink out of the same water fountain as white folks or eat in the same coffee shop. They had to wait to be served in the stores until white folk had been served, but that's just the way things were. I don't think any of those white folks hated anybody enough to hang him from a tree. I couldn't imagine any one of my pa's friends wearing a pointed hood or white robe and burning somebody's house.

A few days after talking to LeRoy, I was sweeping the floor of the store. My pa and I were alone. I had been thinking about what Red and LeRoy had told me. I was trying to figure it out. "Pa," I asked, "Do you know anything about people who wear pointed hoods with white robes and hurt colored people?"

Pa looked at me. "Where did you hear that?"

"Red told me."

"Seems to me Red should be minding his own business. Now you get back to sweeping the floor," Pa said in a tone that meant the discussion was over.

One morning in early August, I woke before dawn. As long as I was awake, I thought I might as well get up and milk our old, tired Jersey cow. I scuffed my way to the barn. Rivers of sweat were running down my back.

I was walking back to the house with a pail full of milk. The rising sun filtered through the muggy air. In the morning haze, I wondered if I was seeing things.

A white-robed person was running down the road at the edge of our land. The face was covered with a white hood.

I hid behind the maple that had shaded our house for years and watched the hooded creature run. All of LeRoy's stories flashed through my mind. My heart drummed in my chest. As I was trying to figure out how to get to the kitchen to protect my ma and the babies, I saw the white-robed person turn in towards my house.

I froze. I looked into the ghastly cutout eye holes on the hood of the creature.

As he ran towards the house, the man stumbled
and the hood lifted up. His face was uncovered.

My pa's face.
My pa was hiding under that hood.
My pa.

As he reached up to pull the hood back down
over his face, my father saw me.

He never spoke to me about that morning.
I never asked. I couldn't find the words.

After that, I still went to the store. I didn't
want to, but I did it.

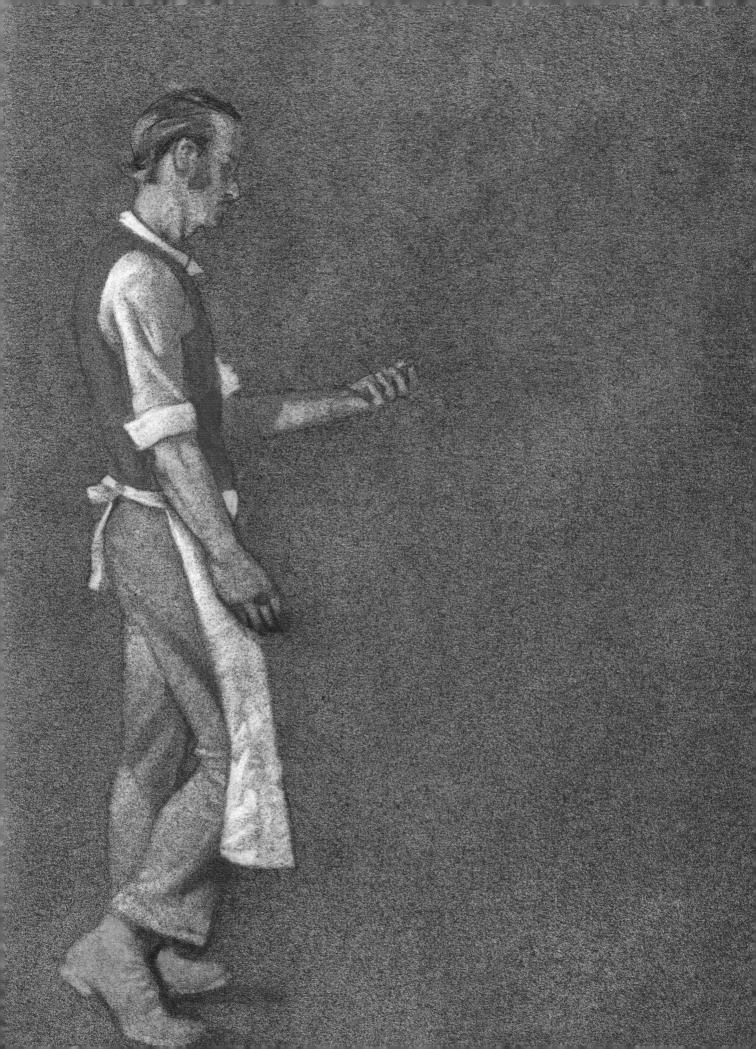

I hung around with Red and fished
occasionally with LeRoy, but somehow
everything was different.

I still loved my pa.
But I never really looked into his
eyes again.
And he never really looked into mine.